© 2023 Amanda J. Clark. All rights reserved.

No portion of this book may be reproduced in any form without written permission from the publisher or author, except as permitted by U.S. copyright law. For permission contact amanda@disciplingwomen.com.

Published by Divine Appointments Publishing
P.O. Box 41
Allardt, TN 38504

ISBN: 979-8-9875377-3-2

Visit the author's website at www.disciplingwomen.com

My momma and dadda must really love kids.
Just when I think our family is complete,
Along comes another and I'm moving to the backseat.

My family is made up of sisters and brothers.
Perfectly imperfect,
None of us better than the others.

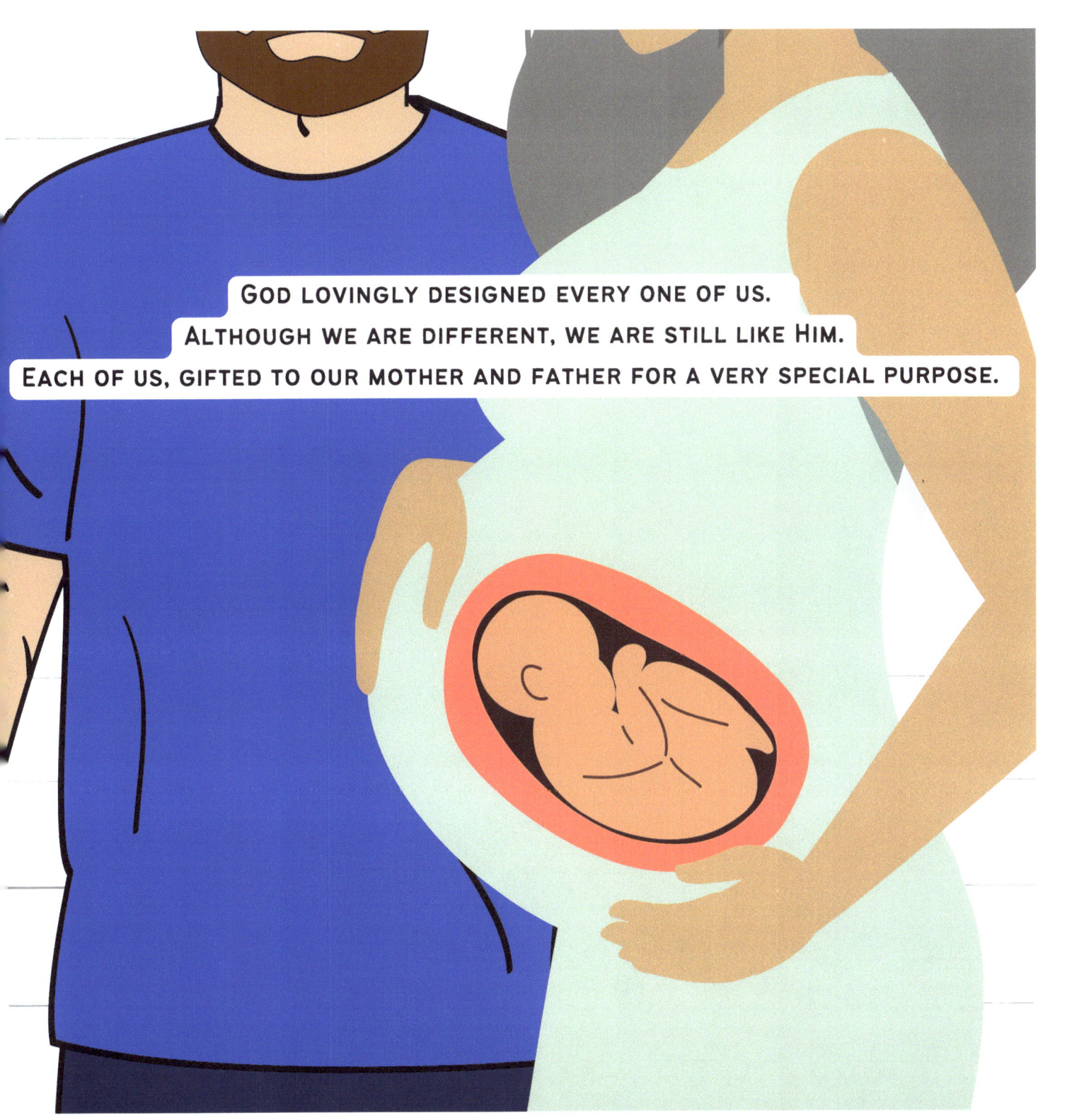

GOD HAS ALWAYS HAD A PLAN—
TO BUILD HIS KINGDOM FOR ETERNITY,
AND TO SHARE HIS LOVE WITH MAN.

WHAT DOES THIS LOVE LOOK LIKE? HOW CAN WE SEE IT?
ONE WAY IS TO GIVE IT AND ANOTHER IS TO RECEIVE IT.

Together every day and together every night,
I don't have to look far for a friend,
or wait too long before a fight.

LOVE COMES EASY MOST DAYS,
BUT I'D BE LYING IF I SAID I LIKE THEM ALWAYS.

Ha Ha Ha!

"Whatever comes and whatever may be,
You are not alone.
God gave you me."

NOTES:

1. Psalm 127: 3-5
2. Romans 3:10, 7:18, and John 13:16
3. Genesis 1:27, Psalm 139:13-14, and James 1:17
4. Psalm 100:3, Hebrews 12:28, Colossians 3:14-17, Revelation 5:13
5. Ephesians 2:5-10, 3:9-11, and Matthew 28:19-20
6. John 13:34-35
7. Galatians 4:6-7
8. Galatians 6:2 and 2 Corinthians 1:7
9. Romans 5:3, Philippians 3:10, and 1 Peter 5:10
10. Philippians 4:7 and 11-12
11. 2 Corinthians 1:4-5
12. Romans 12:9-10 Galatians 6:10
13. Proverbs 17:17
14. Ephesians 5:1, 6:1, 4:32
15. Ephesians 1:5-7
16. Matthew 28:20
17. Philippians 1:6

NOTES

God, please help me to remember all of the ways my brother and sister love me like you.

WWW.DISCIPLINGWOMEN.COM

www.ingramcontent.com/pod-product-compliance
Lightning Source LLC
Chambersburg PA
CBHW041945110426
R18126000001B/R181260PG42743CBX00001B/1